These (dogs) are the partners that find what we can't hear, smell or see, that take the night shift, warn of danger, let us sleep, work hard and rest easy. Bing Bingham's stories awaken something ancient in us as they speak quietly of both duty and deep and lasting regard. He writes to keep appreciation alive for these willing, skilled workers who routinely give us their lives.

- Paul Hunter, author of "Sit a Tall Horse" & "Mr. Brick & the Boys" at www.DavilaBooks.com

Bing Bingham is one of the people who "gets" working dogs. His canine tales will make you laugh out loud or cry, but more than that, they generate a deeper understanding of the dog partners that share their lives with us.

- Cat Urbigkit, author of "Brave and Loyal: An Illustrated Celebration of Livestock Guardian Dogs"

Bing Bingham is a story hound, and he's been gathering good and great dog tales for a long time. He's got a good ear and a great eye for stories that sing and throb. Sitting on the porch with Bing's dog book is sure to make you a smiling time traveler.

- Lynn R. Miller, author of "Art of Working Horses" & "Brown Dwarf" at www.DavilaBooks.com

To know Bing Bingham is to know of his knowledge and life-long love for working dogs. This book is his best yet...I recommend it.

- Jan Jackson, Publisher, Country Traveler Online at www.CountryTravelerOnline.com

Hugging a Dog

True stories from the Dusty Dog Cafe

D. "Bing" Bingham

HUGGING A DOG

Copyright 2022
by D. "Bing" Bingham/Dusty Dog Cafe
All rights reserved.
No part of this book may be reproduced
in any manner without permission
from the publisher.

To obtain consent, contact:
sales@authorzone.link

Printed in the United States of America
First paperback edition, 2023
ISBN: 979-8-98613-310-2

All photography by author
with one exception on page #55
by Ellen Morris Bishop
Design & Layout: Lynn Miller, Eric Grutzmacher,
and Elizabeth Zimmerman
Copy editing: Kema Clark
Website editing: Brin McAtee-Rosenau

This book is dedicated to the people and dogs who walk alongside each other, neither leading nor following, but rather as a matter of trust and respect. May that dance of faith and companionship continue.

- D. "Bing" Bingham

Introduction:

Welcome to the long table at the Dusty Dog Cafe, where the locals gather over a bottomless cup of coffee to swap stories or cuss and discuss the events of their day.

For those of you who've hugged a dog and felt the metronomic beat of their tail against your legs, you'll understand that some of these stories are, much like life, messy. They're covered with dog-hair, slobber, mud, blood and kindness, but they're real. They span the rural American West and travel at the pace of the land...year to year, season to season, birth through death...rather than a human pace. If you're comfortable with that, then top off your mug with another splash of coffee and enjoy the ride.

So, the next question is, where do these stories come from?

In truth they arrive many different ways. We've had phone calls, letters and emails asking if we were interested in a particular story. Sometimes, yes, and other times, not so much.

But, for the most part, they arrive like this one did when I was hanging around the outskirts of a livestock and equipment sale. It was a bright summer day when I ran into a friend I hadn't seen in a couple years. We stepped outside the crowd to catch up on each other's families and lives. Then, he says...

"Ya know, I have a story you might appreciate."

"What's that?" I ask.

He said, "A while back, I was sitting alongside the road talking on my cell phone when an SUV pulled over on the other side of the highway. A guy with a big honkin' camera jumped out."

He went on, "The guy climbed over a barbed wire fence and focused his camera on some chickens pecking around in a pasture. He wasn't paying attention to the big livestock guard dog trotting in his direction, ruff swollen and tail sticking straight in the air."

I knew the place he was talking about. It was a small ranch where they sell meat direct to consumers. Part of their operation includes free-range chickens in mobile enclosures... called 'chicken tractors'...they use the intense pecking of many birds to clean parasites from their fields. When the birds are old enough, they do their part in feeding local families.

"Uh oh," I said.

"Yeah," my friend said, "I yelled to him, but he was concentrating on pointing his camera at the birds and waved me off."

By now, the big dog was in a high trot, coming to investigate the intruder looking at his chickens.

"This time, I yelled…'HEY!'…and pointed to the dog. He ignored me and waved me off again."

"What happened?" I asked.

"I finally yelled…'DOG!!!'…as loud as I could and pointed in its direction. The camera guy turned his head and saw the problem."

Suddenly, the photographer lost interest in chicken pictures. Turning and sprinting for the fence, he crawled at high speed…thoroughly moistened in hot dog breath…back through the barbed wire fence.

"Yeah, there's no way to be graceful while scrambling through a barbed wire fence," he said. "He was all scratched up and bleeding. He glared at me while sliding back in his SUV."

I chuckled, "Yeah, maybe he figured out why there were 'No Trespassing' signs hanging on that fence."

And that, folks, is often how a story ends up in our hands…

> …if that photographer is reading this, we hope he understands that while we laughed at his expense, neither I nor my friend, meant him any harm. That big dog, however, might have been another matter.

*These are the stories of dogs that have made a difference
in the rural American West...*

Chapter One...Gone, Not Forgotten   *11*
- *Willi*
- *Tango*
- *Buck*

Livestock Guardians Cycle – In the Beginning – Part 1   *21*
- *Crimson*
- *Clover*

Chapter Two...Above and Beyond the Call   *25*
- *Cody*
- *Aqui*
- *Molly*

Chapter Three...At the Edge of Their World   *37*
- *Major*
- *Captain Patches*
- *Chloe*

Livestock Guardians Cycle – Hugging a Dog – Part 2   *47*
- *Crimson*
- *Sam*

Chapter Four...A Cry for Help   *53*
- *Atlas*
- *Diesel*
- *Black Dog with No Known Name*
- *Half-Step*
- *Taz*

Livestock Guardians Cycle – Holding a Dog's Head – Part 3   *72*
- *Sam*
- *Keena*
- *Archie*

Chapter Five...Sure Eye, Strong Heart   *80*
- *Boogie*
- *Boogie Again*

CHAPTER ONE
Gone, Not Forgotten

WILLI...

The long table is where the locals gather over a bottomless cup of coffee to swap stories at the Dusty Dog Cafe.

These are stories of working dogs around the rural American West. Whether their job is to take care of their person, dig cranky bulls out of the brush on a daily basis or watch over orphan lambs in a pasture, they carry their weight and ask little of life but a few kibbles, some shelter and an occasional kind word.

Yet the relationship between humans and dogs is more complicated than that. Dogs live, die, thrive or shrivel next to their people, and humans go along for the ride. The dogs in these stories may not have had an easy life, but each made a profound difference in someone's life. The world is a better place because they were here.

This first story is about a dog that shook me to the core and changed my life.

Me and my dog Willi were a team on our tiny and remote ranch. We anticipated each other's thoughts and movement. I hardly needed commands. Most of the time, we could get done what was needed with hand signals and audible tongue clicks.

As our relationship matured and deepened through the years...when I breathed out, she'd breathe in. When she breathed out, I'd breathe in.

However, that didn't mean we agreed on everything...

Me and my aging dog were bickering like an old married couple.

It was a cold, rainy and blustery high desert day. There was nothing comfortable about being outside. I hurried across the yard looking for a staple gun in a tool shed. Out of habit, I absentmindedly called for my dog to follow. Halfway across the yard, I realized she wasn't tagging along.

Turning, I gestured for her to come with me.

However, her body language indicated she wasn't sure this errand was...*really*...that important.

I sighed and gestured again.

She continued to ask with body language, 'Are you sure?'

I could easily stop and force a battle of wills. We both knew who'd win. However, it didn't seem important. After all, the weather was uncomfortable.

Her arthritic hips were aching. I hadn't indicated by my distracted gesture that I...*really*...wanted her to come. She was probably hearing her name called much more clearly by the warm rug next to the toasty wood stove...a very selective type of hearing.

Willi and I have been together since she was born, twelve years previously. We knew each other well, perhaps too well. When I'm frustrated, she usually waits patiently for me to get over it. When I'm distracted, she'll hang out and wait for me to, mentally and emotionally, return to the ranch.

For years, she's been my emotional barometer. When I breathe out, she breathes in. When she breathes out, I breathe in.

My old dog was hurting in the chilly and damp weather. From her point of view, she was asking a legitimate question...'Is what you're doing important enough for me to push through my haze of pain and follow you?'

I thought about it and decided it wasn't.

"Come or don't," I said to her, "but I'm getting out of this rain."

I turned and hurried across the lawn. Moments later, my shadow was hot on my heels. Inside the shed, I paused and gave her a quick pat on the shoulder.

However, our relationship has changed over the years.

She can't jump the way she used to, so I no longer allow her to jump fences. Her job is to guard our ranch ATV and keep marauding sheep and meat goats out of grain buckets. She's increasingly content to sit back and watch the action while the next generation handles the rough stuff.

That's OK with me. I understand. After all, I don't handle the rough stuff like I did when I was young.

She and I have had a good long run. I'm content to spend the time we have left together, whether we're bickering on the porch or watching a winter storm through the window...

...stoked wood stove,
head bobbling and toes toasting
at day's end-
a snoring old dog chases a
tennis ball in pain-free dreams...

...either way, we'll be doing what we've always done best: me breathing out and her breathing in. Her breathing out and me breathing in.

...it was about a year after this story was written when
Willi came to me and explained, in a language we both
understood, that her pain had become too much to bear.
Clear as the north star on a cloudless high desert night,

she asked me for help.

During her life, she gave me everything possible and was my constant friend and companion. I'd never have turned my back on her...nor did I on this day.

My last gift to her was holding her in my arms till she stepped away. Her last gift to me was visiting me in dreams where we do what we always did best...

...me breathing out and her breathing in
her breathing out and me breathing in...

...those are the best dreams.

TANGO...

This next story begins by pointing out there's no good time for a crisis.

Tango is our lead stock dog. He's completely confident of his place in our world and weighs slightly more than a large sack of dog food. When he fixes his amber eyes on a reluctant four-hundred-and-fifty-pound boar hog, there's no doubt who'll win the battle of wills. Yet he's gentle enough to guide a wandering new-born lamb back to its misplaced mother.

Part of any dog's training is socialization with other people. Tango hated being socialized. He'd rather not deal with the public but
was too well behaved to make a fuss. He'd simply slip on his personal...'there's no reason to notice me'...cloaking device for the duration. We had to be careful, or someone would stumble over him if he lay down in the walkway at a public event.

And that's what he was doing, making sure nobody would notice him, when we...ALMOST...had a crisis...

Some years back, my wife and I were sitting behind a folding table selling our specialty sheep's wool.

The show was in a cavernous old wooden barn, stuffed to capacity with nice ladies selling handspun yarn, woven tea towels, knitted scarves, angora sweaters and hats. There were shearling fleeces to snuggle with on a couch, hand-woven rugs, wall hangings and delicate crocheted doilies your grandmother would be proud to display in her living room.

Toward the end of the show, we noticed a man standing just inside the entry door. He was well over six feet tall and built like a retired NFL lineman. He was dressed, head to toe, in black motorcycle leathers. By his looks, he couldn't have been more out of place if he'd stepped into an elegant tea party holding a greasy wrench on a linen napkin. Just one of his well muscled legs weighed more than some of those sweet old grannies.

Neither my wife nor I are quick to jump to conclusions about a person's appearance. Nevertheless, we watched the man move quietly around the room. He'd stop at a booth, ask a few questions, then move on.

Before long, he'd been through most of the show and was standing in front of our booth.

"Can I say 'Hi' to your dog?" he quietly rumbled.

Tango, cloaking device turned up full force, was snoozing beneath our table. Much to his dismay, he was off the ranch getting his socialization skills refresher course.

We were surprised the large man had seen our dog in his hiding place under the table.

Without waiting for a reply, the big man dropped to his knees in the aisle and stuck his head underneath our table. On the floor, he was face to face with Tango. From our side, I could see the startled dog quickly stand.

Tango's neither naturally aggressive nor macho. He's in his prime, can work hard all day or make a snorty bull say 'please' and mind his manners. Loud noises, sudden surprises or much of the human race are not high priorities on his bucket list.

I stood quickly in case I needed to do a quick surgical removal of our dog's teeth from the large fellow's face. We were relieved when no snarls or screams of pain echoed around that big barn from beneath our table.

We're not sure exactly what happened when he and our boss dog suddenly came eye-to-eye. We assume they quickly assessed each other and, within moments, became best buddies.

On our side of the table, Tango's stub tail slowly wagged back and forth until his entire rear end was shimmying in canine joy. On the other side, the big man's great leather clad butt was waggling with the same pleasure. If he'd had a dog's tail, no kneecap in the aisle would have been safe. Soon our folding table was jouncing up and down as man and dog enjoyed each other's company.

Above the table, my wife and I shared a glance. We knew how close we'd been to a crisis.

Eventually, the new best friends under our table

separated. The big man who loves dogs climbed to his feet in front of our booth.

"Thank you," he said, "you've got a good one there."

"We know," we said, sagging slightly with relief.

The large man walked away and headed for the door. The sound of his Harley's exhaust pipes echoed off nearby buildings as he roared off down the highway.

That night, the three of us were glad to get home to our other dogs. A quiet dinner and peaceful evening were just the thing after a wild day at the sale. Tango curled up and relaxed as he slept in the living room between our reading chairs.

...for our part, we never got the large man's name.

A couple decades or so have gone by since this incident. In that time, Tango passed.

However, if by chance, that big man reads this...we'd love to tell him 'Hello' and offer to introduce him to some of our other good dogs.

BUCK...

This story begins with an act of kindness from a gruff old Irish dairyman to an earnest young farm veterinarian whose diagnosis didn't work...and a cow died.

"It's OK, Doc, they die," he said as he patted the vet gently on the shoulder.

That remark of acceptance made an enormous difference for the fresh-out-of school vet who was working hard to find his footing in a remote, rural practice.

Over the years the Irishman and vet became working friends. Sometime later, the dairyman's grandson took an interest in family operation. To that end, he acquired a young stock dog he named Buck.

The dog was working well and the vet enjoyed seeing the dog whenever he was on a farm call. Then one day, the farm vet got a phone call from the Irishman...

Could he come take a look at Buck? Something was wrong with his hindquarters. It seemed like he was partially paralyzed.

A physical and neurological exam showed no indication of injury or nerve damage. Any additional testing was expensive and out of the small-time dairyman's budgetary price range.

So the veterinarian prescribed a course of a pain-blocking medication to relieve the young dog's discomfort and, hopefully, allow him to heal himself. He gave the owner a lengthy list of instructions and sent him home with the dog.

A few days later, the dairyman called back and said there'd been no improvement at all. A busy man, with a dairy to run, he thought it might be time for euthanasia.

By this time the farm vet had grown quite fond of Buck. He'd proven to be a very pleasant and personable dog. He was also interested in the animal's medical condition.

The vet asked, "Would you be willing to give Buck to me and I'll continue to do what I can for him, of course, euthanizing if it becomes necessary?"

The Irishman agreed and the vet took Buck home.

The first thing he did was call in a favor with a human clinic that had a CT scanner. This would give him a much more detailed picture than the x-ray of the dog's afflicted area. After regular business hours, he quietly slipped in the door and tip-toed down the halls carrying Buck in his arms.

Throughout the entire ordeal, Buck was as endearing as ever. However, there was a problem. The results showed nothing. The dog appeared normal on the scans.

It was time for the next step.

The farm vet contacted an outfit across the state specializing in making carts to increase the mobility of dogs with hind-limb paralysis. As it happened, they had one available which had been returned by another client. As a bonus, it had extra big, all terrain tires.

The vet got it in the mail, fitted it to Buck and it took him five minutes to figure it out. He was happily motoring around the veterinary office on his front legs, greeting each employee with a sniff and a lick.

From then on, every morning the vet would load Buck and his cart onto the floor of his pickup, and they'd head to the office. When it came time for farm calls, Buck was loaded back into the truck and off they'd go. Buck would spend the entire farm call bumping around a pasture checking scents and giving anyone he met a sniff and a lick.

Among the far-flung people in the rural American West, communities gather for a variety of different reasons. Many times, these gatherings evolve into a social event where distant neighbors take the time to relax, enjoy a bit of downtime, and catch up with each other's lives. In this region, the blood donation drive was a community event.

Buck would arrive at the blood drive with his veterinary escort and make the rounds, like any small-town political candidate, offering everyone his trademark sniff and lick. He'd approach each person with a soulful look in his eye. If he got a pat on the head, he'd lay his head in their lap and continue his gaze. After a moment of mutual bliss, he'd move on to his next new friend. He continued around the room working the crowd for all it was worth and the people enjoyed the show. If Buck had been a human being, there's no doubt he could have been elected county commissioner.

But there was a problem at home. Whatever had afflicted Buck's nervous system and rear legs ascended to where his front legs began to fail.

There was nothing else to do for him. Lying alone by the fire without being able to get up wouldn't have been much of a life for a dog that's bred to be active. Plus, it would have been marking time until the problem progressed to where he could no longer breathe.

The farm vet and his family said good-bye to Buck while his life was still good, and they laid him to rest in the spot they reserved for other members of their furred family.

...and that's where this story ends: an act of kindness on behalf of a dog that didn't get a fair shake with his health. He did the best he could with what he had for as long as he was able.

LIVESTOCK GUARDIANS CYCLE
In the Beginning – Part 1

CRIMSON and CLOVER

This story begins a couple decades ago when my wife and I got ourselves in trouble.

Every time we turned our flock of sheep and meat goats out on range, between loose dogs and coyotes, we'd lose one of our animals each day. New in the area, we'd been discovered by local predators. Guard donkeys or llamas were of limited success because, all too often, the protector and protectee were on the wrong side of the fence.

Ranching is a business and losing a lamb or goat on occasion is part of the deal. We regard it as a tithe to the local wildlife that share the land. However, when that happens every day, it's like hooking a siphon hose to your bank account and watching your money run out on the ground. It's possible to sustain the loss far a while, but eventually it'll put you out of business and your dreams will evaporate into the high desert breeze.

Our ranch ledgers were looking more than a trifle thin. We needed to decide: dribble our livelihood away or look for help...

That was when my wife spotted an ad for a livestock guard dog breeder's dispersal sale. The breeder had two experienced, sibling sisters who needed a new home. My wife made the call.

We bartered, bargained, and traded for the dogs and finally got the job done. Before long they were in our driveway and seeing their new home from the back of a pickup.

Their names were Clover and Crimson. They were young and strong. Each weighed just under a hundred pounds. As they pulled up to our gate, their eyes were large, round and frightened by their sudden change in circumstances.

We turned them loose in our livestock pens. As expected, the sheep and goats panicked and huddled in a corner. The dogs moved forward with submissive body language hoping to be accepted by this new flock.

As the breeder prepared to return home, she gave us some last-minute bits of advice for working with our new dogs. Plus, she explained the reason for their dispersal.

Apparently, her neighbor put in a new well house and they ended up in a property line dispute. The breeder won and the neighbor needed to change the building location. In a cruel twist of vengeance, her neighbor began firing his shotgun in the air every time he saw her dogs in the fields. With no property damage or physically injured animals, there was nothing the authorities could do.

She said, "Toward the end, my proven guard dogs would run cringing to the house every time they heard gunfire. For their sake and mine, I decided to sell out and move away."

As she pulled her pickup back on the road headed for her unhappy home, my wife and I looked at each other. We were both wondering what we'd gotten ourselves into and thinking there's a very special spot in Hell for a man who takes his revenge out on dogs that had nothing to do with his problem. Nevertheless, we were still in a tough spot and needed to find a way to make a difficult situation work.

We held our flock in a large pen for a few weeks while canines and critters got acquainted. There was some jostling and bawling, but no injuries. At night, both dogs would hop the fence and check out their new territory. They left their scent marks in all the proper places, announcing to local predators there was a new sheriff in town, so to speak.

At the time, livestock guard dogs were new in the Pacific Northwest. Some breeders had a theory the dogs should be handled and socialized as little as possible. And since we were new to this too, we weren't sure what was happening when neither of the dogs approached or wanted anything to do with us during feeding at evening chores. We weren't comfortable with the situation and didn't know what we didn't know about them or their training. We worked with what we had.

Soon the guard dog sisters learned and adapted to the ways of our ranch. We turned them out on range with our flock.

They knew their business and had a strategy. Crimson, the larger of the two, was the outrider and intimidator. Clover stayed close and covered the flock.

Our predator problems dried up.

One morning at turnout time, the sisters were gone. We made frantic phone calls to the neighbors. They'd seen nothing. Then, a couple days later, word came from a dozen miles away that our dogs had been spotted deep in the desert canyons. They were busy harassing a cougar out of our region.

We were glad they were alive. At the news, my wife and I did a 'high-five' as we passed each other in the hallway.

A day and a half later Clover, the homebody, returned and took up her post with the flock. Her sister Crimson, the enforcer, arrived the next evening, limping badly. Both were exhausted, thirsty and glad to be back with their flock.

We fed the dogs well, let them rest and spoke our gratitude for moving the big cat out of the neighborhood. Neither allowed us to touch them. We put down their food on the ground and stepped back before they'd eat.

All went well for a year. Predator problems were down and meat prices up. We weren't getting rich, but our ledger was on the mend.

Later that year, as the Fall storms gathered, Clover returned from her rounds. But there was a problem. She was lying on her side in the middle of our pens and wouldn't eat. We couldn't tell if she was sick or injured as she lay whimpering quietly. We had no idea if she'd consumed something poisonous, had an internal injury from a fight with a predator or was the victim of a rattlesnake bite. We tried to help, each time we approached, she'd growl at us and crawl off, crying piteously...

...hoping and helpless,
I watch, with hands in pockets,
her shattering pain –
her sister whines quietly
in shared distress...

...we didn't have many options and only a fool will force himself on an injured dog capable of intimidating cougars.

Meanwhile, Crimson stood guard and worried over her sister. Her weight shifting constantly between front paws. She wanted help for her sister but allowed no one to provide it.

Late that night, hoping the problem was a case of serious indigestion and would work itself out, we returned to the house. We phoned everyone who might have an idea that would help our dog. Nothing, no one had ever heard of the situation. We didn't sleep much that night.

First light, we found Clover dead in our livestock pens.

Crimson was still guarding her sister. Using body language, we asked her permission to touch Clover's body. She assented by turning her head aside.

Clover had been killed by an old snare. Somehow, the huge dog dived through a tiny opening meant for a 25-pound coyote and had been snared around her upper abdomen. As she struggled to break the trap, the cable tightened, slowly crushing her heart. It was a hard end for a dog who deserved better.

We didn't sleep much the next night, either...

...Clover's death was difficult to watch. Especially so, since the dog's fear prevented even the briefest touch; one that would have allowed us to find a pair of wire cutters.

Life and death are a process. It's not personal. However, that doesn't mean it's acceptable to be callous or cynical. We acknowledged and accepted our grief. Then we promised ourselves we'd continue to do our best with the tools we had to hand.

In the following days, our ranch was a very quiet place.

Still grieving, Crimson took up her sister's slack with our flock. She did an excellent job. If one of our animals was in trouble, she'd attract our attention and wait nearby for us to handle the matter.

Still, she never allowed herself to be touched.

[to be continued on page 47]

CHAPTER TWO
Above and Beyond the Call

CODY...

This story begins in the late fall during a stormy week. Regular rain squalls, one after another, raked the land like a giant harrow. The mud in the cattle feedlot was the stuff of legend. Livestock feeding chores, rescuing stuck vehicles, and relocating rubber boots that'd been sucked from a sock-covered foot into the thick goo were the day's work.

On this day, almost everyone had gladly gone home for the weekend. Jeff and his dog Cody were the only ones on duty when the late grain shipment arrived. The truck driver was anxious to go home.

Together, they offloaded the grain in record time. Running before the next squall, Jeff ground the grain. The only thing between him and a weekend in his warm house was a quick cleanup of the grinder...

Standing on the edge, Jeff was kicking the last of the grain into the hopper when his footing disappeared, and his left leg sank to the knee.

His foot was hit by the spinning grinder blade.

Adrenaline surging, he threw himself backward out of the hopper and landed on the ground. Sitting upright, he saw his left leg was gone below the knee and bright red arterial blood fountained into the mud.

He was in trouble.

Jeff ripped a strip from his shirt and tightened a tourniquet around his leg stump. Still, blood dribbled. Crawling on two hands and one knee through the driving rain, he wobbled toward his pickup hoping to find help.

Trauma and blood loss dropped him over the edge into shock. Clear thought patterns disappeared. Furiously jabbing his only remaining foot, back and forth, between gas pedal, brake and clutch, he managed to spin the truck's tires, miring it in the cold mud.

More frightened and alone than he'd ever been in his life, Jeff opened the door and dropped on his three working limbs into a cold puddle. He set off on a marathon crawl for the only phone in the feedlot, leaving tracks through the muck...

...scratched in the mud
in hieroglyphs of pain, the trail
leads into the night –
only a dog saw how badly
he wanted to live...

...in a red haze of pain, Jeff passed out.

After a time, he slowly resurfaced into consciousness and stared, barely understanding, his sodden surroundings. Cody was there, standing over him, frantically licking his muddy face.

Jeff continued his soggy crawl toward the office phone while his strength and determination were dribbling into the freezing mud. Each time he passed out, Cody was there... desperately...licking his face until he awakened and crawled off.

After what seemed like an eternity, covered in mud and blood, Jeff reached the office. His thought processes were intermittent. His breathing, shallow and rapid. It was difficult to focus his eyes. Somehow, he dialed 911 and spoke into the phone.

Then, he sprawled back on the floor, passing in and out of consciousness. Each time he slipped back into the dank mud of unconsciousness, Cody leaped into a face-licking frenzy. Back and forth, they went...conscious and unconscious, frantic face-licking and worried watching through what seemed like an endless night. His only memory was of a dog tongue .. .lickingandlickingandlicking...as fast as it could go.

The paramedics arrived and raced into the night to the hospital.

...it took a year or so for Jeff to gather the pieces of his
life into one spot. During the day, he learned about

the frustrations of fitting his new prosthetic leg to his old stump and dealt with worries about the future of a one-legged cowboy. At night, grisly scenes and ghosts haunted his dreams.

But, like that terrible night, those problems worked out.

These days, Jeff drives a pickup with an automatic transmission. He and Cody spend their summers keeping an eye on yearling cattle. During winter, they watch over 300 mother cows busy with calving. They do the same work as other cowboys, just slower.

Jeff realizes Cody saved his life on that terrible rainy night. He's sure there's no way to express every ounce of gratitude to his buddy. But that seems to be OK with Cody. He's happy doing what stock dogs do.

Besides that, since the accident, Jeff lets him sleep in the house...

*...a dog's soft rug,
near a popping wood stove
next to your chair
and our quiet breathing -
our world, you and I...*

...we suspect Cody knows about gratitude.

AQUI...

Springtime in the desert.

New life is everywhere. Meadowlarks are claiming territory and daring anyone to intrude. Lomatium and wild parsley dot the land with the new growing season's nutrients, and coyote pups are taking their first steps outside the den. In ranch country, it means weaning calves as the grass grows.

Stock dogs have their own job description when the year's new growth arrives. Soon calves will be branded, turned out on range and need to be moved to new pastures.

However, sometimes there's parts of their job not included in their contract's fine print.

The first thing most people notice about Aqui is her eyes, some call them 'Wise Eyes.'

No one knows much about her breeding. She's a generic Indian reservation stock dog, large enough to intimidate a cranky cow, yet small enough to ride easily in the pickup's jump seat. Some folks say there's a touch of coyote in her distant background.

Aqui and the old rancher are best buddies. She shadows him constantly, from the time he arises until he totters off to bed. No leash is necessary. If he's on horseback, she's tucked in near his stirrup. If he's afoot, she's walking alongside...

It was calving season and the old rancher was recovering from a pulled hamstring muscle. Nothing serious, but it hurt like the dickens. Every day, he managed chores, but it was slow going.

On this day, he spotted a newborn calf snoozing in the spring sunshine. The cow, hard work of a successful birth completed, nibbled on grass a hundred feet away. All looked to be the way it should be.

But the old rancher was curious. He thought this might be a good time to take a peek and determine the sex of the calf.

Limping along, he climbed through the fence into the pasture. Knowing cattle are sometimes protective of their young, he kept an eye on the cow while hobbling along. Unfazed, mama munched on her grass while her little one dreamed of warm milk and sunny pastures.

Groaning, the old rancher stooped and lifted the calf's hind leg.

"A healthy heifer," he thought, slowly backing toward the fence.

That's when the calf woke up.

A newborn calf is a bleary-eyed animal that locates its mother by smell and sensing movement. The smell of this calf's mother was all around in the gentle breeze. Feeling the need to

nurse, the confused little animal's eyes followed the first moving blur it could find...the old rancher hobbling toward the fence.

Then several things happened very quickly...

The calf, seeking sustenance and maternal nurturing, climbed to its unsteady feet and followed the old rancher.

The cow, seeing her newborn calf wobbling off in the wrong direction, fixed her protective eye on the slowly moving mini parade.

The old rancher, realizing a problem was developing, limped faster.

Then, the calf, thinking her mother was moving away, bawled her distress. The cow, fearing for her frightened little one, pawed the ground and made a full-speed, mother-bear style protective run at the rancher.

In that instant, the old rancher knew with absolute clarity that he was about to be bottom plowed into a bloody smear across his own field.

That's when Aqui, lounging in the nearby shade, lifted her head to pay attention to the unfolding situation. Like a hunting cheetah, she closed on the mad mother cow...the fight was on.

Leaping into the air, she locked her jaws on the cow's tender nose. Furious, the cow bellowed, slinging snot, saliva, and dog back and forth as she raced around the pasture. Aqui tightened her grip and hung on while she was being used in the bovine version of Crack-The-Canine-Whip.

Meanwhile, the old rancher, unable to do anything to help his dog in her precarious situation, completed his hobbling retreat and climbed to safety.

That was the signal for Aqui to drop off the cow's nose and scuttle through the fence. Then the angry cow hurried to her confused calf offering maternal consolation.

Back in the house, the rancher's relieved wife...who'd witnessed the entire incident...decided it might be a good thing for him to take the rest of the day off so his leg could heal.

The old rancher was fine with relaxing in his easy chair, leg on a stool.

...a couple weeks later, yours truly, was visiting the old rancher. Aqui was sitting by his side while he rested his hand on her head.

I asked, "So, how do you feel about Aqui, now that she's saved your bacon?"

"You know," he drawled, "I wasn't looking for a dog when I got this one, but she's about 97 percent perfection in a good dog...if someone had trimmed her dewclaws so they didn't get caught in the brush, she'd have been an even 98 percent."

So, there you go, folks, now you know... wink-wink...what it takes to be a good dog in the rural American West.

By the way, during our entire conversation, Aqui rested her head on the old rancher's lap and soaked it all in. As long as he was there, she was fine, and it didn't matter to her what we talked about.

MOLLY...

It's not uncommon for a loyal dog to assist their owner in a difficult situation. However, most of the time the owner has a pretty good idea about what the dog is doing. But, that's not always the case.

Her neighbors call her 'Old Lona.' Some say she's barely bigger than a bar of soap. just over five feet tall and, maybe, outweighing a hundred-pound sack of chicken scratch. This octogenarian lives alone, deep in the desert, with her cattle, range horses and beloved dog.

Molly is a young livestock guard dog who weighs only slightly more than her owner. At night she sits vigil on a nearby hill overlooking the house where anything moving can be seen.

During the day, dog and owner aren't far apart. Where one goes, the other is nearby.

When Molly gets bored, she does her best to entice Lona into a game of Work-Glove-Keep-Away by snitching the glove from the pocket of her work jacket and standing in front of her, cross-bodied, while looking back expectantly over her shoulder.

"I don't want to play, you silly dog," says Lona while ruffling the canine ears.

However, when a working dog knows her job of protecting everything and everyone in her territory and she does it by outsmarting her owner, confusion happens...

Lona worries about her livestock. On this day she was concerned about a missing heifer with a brand-new calf. They hadn't showed up at the usual time.

Just before bedtime, she stepped outside to take a last look around. There was no sign of the bovine pair. Unable to sleep, there wasn't much she could do but sip her nighttime tea and worry.

Later that night, still unable to sleep, she climbed out of bed. It was a soft and lovely summer night. She grabbed

her flashlight. Dressed only in a nightgown and raggedy tenny runners, Lona stepped out the door hoping to spot that young cow. Nothing. She stepped out into the dark.

Molly stretched in her bed under a juniper tree and trotted along behind.

Two hours later, still searching, Lona was edging around a brush pile when she stumbled on an old tangle of barbed wire and fell into a rock pile. Not seriously injured, she'd badly bruised her gimpy shoulder and was unable to use her arms to get back on her feet. No matter which way she twisted or rolled, every time she tried to stand, no luck.

Molly watched the process. She waited for her moment, then stepped in front of Lona, stood cross-bodied, and looked back expectantly.

"I don't have time to play!!" Lona yelled, frustrated tears streaming. She pushed the dog away.

It's a quiet and creeping vulnerability that builds to an overwhelming wave when an aging and partially clad woman is incapacitated and...no one, but her...knows where she is. Panic saps vital energy as it seeps into the widening cracks of a strong personality.

Not one to give up, Lona tried to rise again. Molly blocked her crosswise and looked back over her shoulder. Lona was weakening. Sobbing with fear and frustration, still sitting in the rocks she rested one hand on the dog's shoulder. Molly immediately spread her front paws and braced herself.

Lona paused and took a deep breath. She experimented. With her good arm, she wriggled and squirmed into a kneeling position. Then, leaning heavily on the dog's shoulders, she wobbled to her feet.

Balancing Lona by standing still, Molly displayed a toothy grin. Then, slower than a snail makes its trail, they tottered toward home, with Molly acting as a furry crutch.

Hours later, before dawn, safe in her doorway, Lona hugged her dog, "I didn't understand what you were trying to tell me, I'm sorry."

Then, she fixed herself a mug of hot tea and plunked down in her favorite rocker. As her fear and adrenaline subsided, her body relaxed, and her head drooped. She drifted into a much-needed sleep.

Lona's tea was cold beside her chair when first light touched the living room window. She opened the front door and spotted the missing heifer and a healthy calf grazing on her front lawn. Slowly, she made her way over to where Molly was snoozing in the lilacs. With her one good arm, she hugged her dog again, whispering, "thank you."

These days, Lona's scrapes, gouges, and sore shoulder are healing. Every so often, she'll pause in the day's work and give Molly a hug.

"Thank you for being there," she says.

For Molly's part, she's not confused about her new abundance of one-armed hugs. She's adapting just fine to the extra attention.

For her, the important thing is that she and Lona are together and there's always more work gloves to snitch.

...about three years after this story took place, Lona passed. Her death was peaceful and not unexpected.

But it ripped the roots out of Molly's life.

Since that time, Molly has found a new home. Her owners love her and gave her a job to do. Now she guards piglets from desert predators and wandering neighbor dogs.

At this writing, Molly is still grieving the loss of Lona. But she's showing signs of adapting to her new life with Paul and Leslie.

To keep the dog from wandering in search of her long-lost friend, the new owners tied her near the pigpens as she watches over her new charges. She's adopted an old horse trailer...complete with humongous dog bed...as her very own house. This gives her plenty of shade in the summer and a break from the howling winter wind.

About two months after Molly moved to her new home, Paul and Leslie were away from the farm when they got a frantic call from their caretaker.

"Molly's been doing a lot of barking so I went out to check and she's broken her chain and disappeared!!" he said.

Neither Paul nor Leslie were sure what to do or where the dog would go. An hour later, they received a much calmer phone call.

"Good news," the caretaker said, "I found Molly, but she's got blood all over her muzzle. I think

she killed a coyote that was trying to get into the piglets."

Molly is still having a tough time with her grief, but new owners and dog are working out their differences. Maybe best of all, she has a job to do and pigs to guard.

So folks, please send a good-hearted, hard-working dog a kind thought or gentle prayer. She's trying her best to make a way in this world and would likely appreciate it.

CHAPTER 3
At the Edge of Their World

MAJOR...

On a good night, Kyal sleeps well.

When a bad night happens, his dreams devolve into nightmares. The details of each one is different, but the theme is always the same: blood, pain, gore, and violence...all the things you'd expect from a military veteran with post-traumatic stress who's served in a theater of war.

Just as the pain and fear threaten to overwhelm him, he feels a tiny and gentle lick on the end of his nose. If that strange sensation, amidst the violence, doesn't bring him out of his nightmare then he'll feel a second gentle lick.

Most times, the second lick is right on target at the end of his nose. But, sometimes, they're off-center and he'll get a swipe of a tongue across his closed eyelid or a slurp that'll end up in his hair.

That's when Kyal opens his eyes and steps out of the violence into a moment of calm and safety staring into the eyes of Major, his PTSD service dog.

From within that moment, there's no longer any need for fear and pain. There's just Kyal and Major...eye to eye and nose to nose...holding on to each other in a moment of comfort.

But it took more than a few miles of travel for Major to find Kyal...

Major was a standout in this Wyoming litter of pups. He was lighter colored than the others, almost white, and had one tiny dark spot on the left side of his nose.

At weaning time, as it does for all service animal prospects, their personalities were evaluated and three, including Major, were selected and their training began. In a freak accident, Major was seriously injured, and the volunteer efforts of a local veterinarian put him on the road to recovery. Once again his personality was evaluated and there were no lingering psychological effects. He worked his way through service dog training with flying colors and his winning personality.

After all, Major was a young dog that had places to go and a job to do.

Major was just short of two years old when his call came to serve Mickey, a struggling Vietnam veteran.

The two hit it off and Mickey's 50-year-old ghosts loosened their grip on his heart and mind. He smiled again. And, best of all, he could go out in public and enjoy his family once more.

Then five months later, Mickey opened his front door one evening to step outside. That's where he took his final breath. Only Major knows exactly what happened next as his person suddenly passed away.

The next morning Mickey's worried daughter found her deceased father covered in light colored dog hair with Major hovering over him. She figures the dog must have spent the night trying to revive him.

She said, "I think my father died happier than he'd been in a long time because his buddy was with him to the end."

In most cases, where the veteran passes before his service dog, the family is offered the animal because of the strong bonds that are built between them.

This time, because Major was barely over two years old, Mickey's daughter requested the dog be given an opportunity to help someone else the way he'd given her father hope.

And that's when Kyal got the phone call...

...and Major stepped in, with tiny nose licks, to bridge the gap in Kyal's life.

One of Kyal's most outstanding traits is his voice. He could probably pitch it to be heard in just about any combat situation. But that doesn't mean he's comfortable talking in public.

Kyal and Major attended Mickey's funeral. They'd never met, neither veteran knew the other.

He got up in front of the crowd and explained

who he was and how grateful he was that Major had come into his life...not because of Mickey's death...but because his family decided to pass along the healing to another veteran who was having a tough time.

He finished his brief speech by saying..."I'm here today to support Mickey and his family, because through Major I feel like I'm part of that family."

"You are!" the crowd yelled and applauded.

During the whole time, Major quietly watched Kyal as he returned to his chair.

These days Kyal and Major are a team as they move around their Oregon home. Kyal still has tough days, but his PTSD symptoms have been reduced to about 25% of what they were before Major came into his life.

When those hard days return, both Kyal and Major look forward to their shared moment of comfort.

CAPTAIN PATCHES...

*Hospice is a fragile time for folks who are
steadily losing, drip by drip, everything they used
to know and understand. One by one, their physical
activities are given up while they emotionally prepare
themselves for their demise.*
*According to the former Archbishop Emeritus
Desmond Tutu...'A person is a person through other
persons.' When someone loses contact, for whatever
reason, from other people they know and recognize, some
of their humanity slips away...*

Rob and Captain Patches are trained hospice volunteers.
They've been doing it for many years. One thing they've learned
over time is it's better not to argue with little old ladies, but
rather let them have their dance.

On a good day, this woman would chat and swap stories.
A bad day meant she could barely move a hand or her arm. For
her, quality of life meant a visit from Hospice volunteers, Rob
and therapy dog Captain Patches.

In most cases, Rob wouldn't allow his canine star-of-the-
show on the bed. For this woman he made an exception. From
the moment they walked in the room she would continually be
patting and loving on his 60-pound rescue dog. During the entire
session her husband sat smiling quietly in his appointed chair on
the other side of the room.

"Can I have Captain Patches?" she'd coo. "Can he stay
with me?"

Each time Rob patiently explained that his dog had other
hospice patients to visit and it was important Captain Patches
stay with him to get the work done.

The dog ownership dance between Rob and this woman
continued through that spring into a hot summer. Each visit
found her husband dutifully sitting quietly across the room with
a fan blowing cooling air over her.

One day Rob walked in for a visit, Captain Patches in tow. She beamed and patted the bed where the dog regularly sat. When all were comfortable, the ownership tango began...

"I'd really like it if Captain Patches could stay with me," she said.

"Well, you know..." Rob began.

That's when she started rapidly batting her eyes in Rob's direction.

Rob paused; he wasn't sure what to do. He recognized she was flirting and upping her game in acquiring his dog. She sweetened her offer.

"If you'll let me keep Captain Patches, you can have my favorite possession," she offered, her gaze lighting on the cooling fan.

"I really couldn't..." he stated.

Eyelids still fluttering in his direction, she aimed a smile at Rob and ratcheted up her offer again:

"You can have my husband, too. He's a really good worker."

Gently, Rob smiled.

"I'm sure he is, but there's nowhere for Captain Patches to sleep here," he said, thinking quickly. "Besides, he really does need to see other people."

Slowly, gracefully, Rob said goodbye to the lonely woman who was facing the end of her life. He made his way down the hall to the next hospice patient.

The following week they stopped by her room, again. She was glad to see them and continued the dog ownership dance.

As longtime hospice volunteers, Rob knows he and Captain Patches begin their work the moment they arrive on a motorcycle with sidecar: he pauses in the parking lot to help the dog out of his protective eye wear. Then, flower bouquet in hand, they march into the building where Captain Patches steals the show. Like closed flowers on a chilly spring day, the residents open to receive the sunshine of the dog's unconditional love and acceptance. Smiles bloom around the room.

But to suppose a dog gets nothing out of the deal would be a mistake. Years back when Captain Patches was a youngster and Rob was starting out, they visited a man whose wife was in an assisted living center.

The man was thrilled with the visits. He loved dogs. He and Rob had much in common with their mutual love of all things canine. Rob continued visiting.

However, the man's wife was uninterested. For two years of regular visits neither Rob nor Captain Patches interacted with her. She had little or no emotional response. Eventually the man passed and left his wife alone in the facility. One day on a whim, the duo stopped by to check on her.

She looked up with interest. Then she reached out to pet Captain Patches. Slowly she made tentative conversation with Rob. Haltingly they talked about her life.

Over the next months, visits continued. Captain Patches acted as catalyst for the budding friendship. Conversation was no longer strained. Slowly, Rob realized that every time they entered this facility, the dog bee-lined straight to her room.

A couple years passed.

Eventually, so did their friend.

For a year afterward, each time the duo entered that building, Captain Patches led the way to her room, checking to see if his friend had returned.

No one knows what triggered this woman's withdrawal from her life and humanity. However, when that happens, the return road is long and difficult. Outside assistance is imperative.

"Captain Patches helped her bridge that gap," Rob says. "He helped her return to her humanity. It's not easy for a human not to be human. To return, well, that's remarkable."

Her joy of living, once lost, and now returned. There's really not much more to say about a dog except maybe to make sure he gets respect for a job well done.

Ohhhh...and make sure to give him a good ear rub now and then. Rob takes care of that.

> *...Captain Patches is aging.*
> *One day it'll be his turn to step through the veil. To that end, Rob has acquired Lambeau, a puppy, who's gentle, loves people and other dogs, to step into*

Captain Patches' shoes when the event arrives.

However, Rob wants something made very clear...

"I don't want to diminish the end of Captain Patches' life with a puppy taking all the attention and driving him crazy."

That's why Lambeau doesn't get to ride in the motorcycle's sidecar until the senior dog no longer has a need. In everything else, Rob and the junior dog have worked out where each is getting their share of love.

An aging dog getting the respect he deserves seems a fitting finale after he's helped a couple thousand people find their best possible path at the end of their life's journey.

CHLOE...

This next story starts just before the holidays.
Winter storms were building in the Pacific
Ocean. One by one, they slammed into the West Coast.
Snow piled up in the Cascade Mountains while howling
winds raked the passes. Elk and deer hightailed it for the
lowlands and cougars kegged up for the duration in their
dens.

Anyone or anything, with any sense, was
hurrying to get under cover.

Except for those who have none. They do the
best they can under the circumstances.

At the Shepherd's House, a shelter for men in
some of life's most difficult transitions, Chloe, the canine
household greeter, sits by the door...

She's watching hungry people line up at the serving
table. As they file by she sees a problem. Like a hungry coyote
spotting a lagging lamb near the rear of the flock, she ducks and
dodges through the mayhem across the crowded dining room.

One man sits alone at a table. No one knows where
he came from or how long he's been sleeping in the desert. He
might have been driven there for any number of reasons...drugs,
alcohol, PTSD, or mental illness. He's a solitary man living alone
on the edge of the civilized world.

During invocation Chloe sits underneath the table beside
the lone man's leg. As the meal begins, she leans her head on his
thigh. Ignoring her, he shovels down his warm food.

Not willing to take 'no' for an answer, Chloe slips her
nose underneath his hand allowing him to feel her soft, black fur.
Surprised in mid-gobble, the man glances down, as if seeing her
for the first time. He quickly jerks his hand back to his thigh.

More forcefully, she inserts her nose underneath his hand
and flips it to the tip of her ear, distracting him from his much-
needed meal. Startled and embarrassed, the man yanks his hand
back to his thigh while glancing nervously around the table.

After dinner, quiet, sated conversation dominates the dining room. The lone man is silent, avoiding human contact. Pressing her point, Chloe leans harder on his leg.

Touch is a basic human need, essential to emotional health. Deprived of human contact, at best, our emotional balance tips and we retreat into ourselves. At worst, our state of mind tilts till dangerously skewed. Without touch, we become something less.

A couple years previously, the Shepherd's House board of directors decided to add a dog to their toolbox of aid for men in crisis. The next day, the house manager got a call about an animal that needed more TLC than she was getting in her previous home.

Chloe, the newest homeless shelter volunteer and a former outside dog, was terrified at first. As the only female resident in the building she slowly adapted to the needs of the men around her. Before long, with unerring accuracy, she could spot those most in need of unconditional acceptance.

"She brings joy to the guys, it's a big job," says the house manager.

It's nearing 'lights-out' at the Shepherd's House and conversation is dying in the dining room. Contagious jaw-wrenching yawns circulate each table. The emergency residents seeking shelter from the storm make their way into the chapel and find a spot for their floor mats.

The lone man, his humanity still untethered, takes his mat, and moves it in a corner as far as possible from the others. Chloe follows him into the chapel, clinging like a canine bumper sticker and lays beside him. Long after the lights have gone out and the shelter chatter ceases, the lonely man...hesitantly... reaches out and cups Chloe's head with his hand.

Chloe relaxes and leans into his touch...

...humanity's tiny flame,
guttering in the freezing wind:
"I can't feel myself,
does anyone know me?" he cries –
reach, solitary one, we remember you...

...on this dark and frigid evening, a tiny and tentative candle of humanity burns incrementally brighter. For tonight, there is a little more trembling and gentle joy in the world.

Chloe kept up her gentle and healing ministrations of forgotten people for years. Toward the end, her hips and hind legs could no longer hold her up. It became apparent her time had come.

Returning to the Shepherd's House for the final time, the house manager stopped by a nursery and bought an apple tree. There, in the roots, Chloe's ashes were buried for the final time in the front yard.

It took some time, but another dog took up Chloe's position as greeter for homeless people seeking shelter from the storm.

LIVESTOCK GUARDIANS CYCLE
Hugging a Dog – Part 2

CRIMSON and SAM

After confronting the realities of an untouchable and injured livestock guard dog, we figured prevention might be our next best approach.

Retraining Crimson from her fear of being touched was high on the 'To Do' list. Our veterinarian suggested we try canine tranquilizer.

The plan was to slip a dose into Crimson's favorite food. Hopefully, she'd relax and we could chain her. Then, much like gentling a terrified wild animal, we'd work to build bonds of trust...

On the big day Crimson gobbled her hot dogs.

Quietly, we waited for the drugs to take effect. At the first sign of a wobble in her step, we gently walked in her direction, and she staggered to the other side of our large pen. Body language is everything in situations like this. If she thought we were chasing her, it wastes our time and ratchets up her fear response. Not helpful at all.

We exited the pen, leaving more hot dogs with another jumped-up dose of tranquilizer. Curious, but cautious, Crimson investigated. Satisfied, she gulped them down. Once again, submissive body language on display, we slowly re-entered the gate.

Watching and wary, she staggered to her feet and weaved to the far side of the pen. We paused, then coaxed with more hot dogs. Suspicious, she staggered further away.

We held a quick conference and decided to try another dose. This was a delicate decision because too much tranquilizer could stop her heart and breathing. This time we waited until she was sound asleep.

All went well, until we were within ten feet. Some tiny sound must have awakened her, spiking her fear and adrenaline.

Struggling upright, she fled, bouncing off metal feeders, as quickly as she could wobble.

That was my chance. As she stumbled within a few feet of me, I could have made a quick dash and tackled her. But I paused, there were too many questions rattling around my brain.

First, as a middle-aged man, do I have any business trying to overpower a dog that has sent full-grown cougars running for cover? Especially when she's had a triple dose of tranquilizer and not in her right mind?

That sounded like an injury...for either or both of us... waiting to happen. Then I asked myself how far was I willing to go with a terrified animal to make sure that we...not her...didn't have another bad experience with the death of a dog? Dominance with primitive breed dogs is important. However, inflicting myself on an incapacitated and frightened animal, without an overwhelming benefit for it, is another thing entirely.

And that led to a third question: Was this confrontation about me or her? Empathy and emotional resonance with an animal in trouble is one thing. But there are limits. Empathy without bounds or common sense can twist an act to be needlessly cruel for the animal.

I paused and waited while she wobbled away.

It took a few days, but Crimson re-established her relationship...if not her trust...with us. Still, it's hard to look at an emotionally damaged dog and not admit some personal complicity. It's not a flattering vision.

Crimson returned to her job of keeping the predators at bay. Each day, when she returned from the range, we'd make sure she was safe and uninjured in the pens. We put out her food and she'd eat after we backed away. Touching her was out of the question.

All went as well as could be expected for a couple years.

However, Crimson's graying muzzle and sagging eyes were showing her age. In the ranch business, it's a well-known training tactic to let a young dog learn the job from a senior, more experienced animal. Hoping that Crimson would teach a youngster the ways of our flock and the predatory ropes in our neighborhood, we bought a young guard dog pup.

His name became Sam.

Once again, Crimson did a great job. She showed him all her scent posts, overlooks for viewing large areas, cooling water holes and the best places to snitch a bit of carrion for a snack in the shade.

What Sam didn't learn from her was eating habits.

Every evening, he happily greeted us for food. When finished, he'd do his best to climb into our laps for attention. Crimson would watch his antics for a moment, then find herself a comfortable spot in the straw for an evening snooze.

The following spring, as we turned our flock out on range, both Crimson and Sam were on full-time guard duty. The new kid in the neighborhood showed promise and tagged along on their rounds with a big, toothy grin. She had the posture of an elderly dog, her rheumy eyes no longer picking out important details.

Each time the duo trotted out the gate with flock in tow, she appeared as a happy old dog. In the evening, she'd return tired and ready for food.

We modified our expectations and figured if it was her time to pass, we'd accept it and do the best we could with whatever presented itself. However, in our hearts, we hoped things would change and we'd get a chance to hug her big head and feel her tail beating against our legs. We knew it was probably more than we'd get. Still, we hoped.

That fall, our lives changed once again. We began building a new house. Big trucks delivered supplies. Backhoes scooped foundations and framing crews of loud-talking, fast-moving men were the order of the day. People hollered, radios played, and saws turned long lumber into shorter pieces. It was a busy and chaotic time.

Sam adapted to the new situation and took it in stride. Crimson didn't understand. For her, our world was increasingly uncomfortable. She grew frantic and withdrew further, refusing any attempts at reassurance.

Then the attacks started.

One busy day, my wife took our three herding dogs out for chores. Just inside the gate, unprovoked, hundred pound Crimson pounced on my thirty-pound Boogie. The fight was nothing like fair. It was an ambush and attempted killing. We used stock whips and wrist-thick tree branches to break up the melee.

Boogie survived, barely.

Our veterinarian said, "Your dog's been given a kill-shake like a rat. She's not seriously wounded, but it'll be up to her to decide if she wants to live. To be honest, at this moment, she's not sure if living is worth the trouble."

Her physical injuries were minimal. No broken bones or open wounds, and her internal bruising was survivable. It was her will to live that was damaged. She and I spent that night on the floor, lying next to each other...

...my hand on her hip,
we spoke in whispers and silence.
"Stay or step away,
if you leave, I'll miss you, but understand" –
exhausted dog groans punctuate the night...

...as the next morning's sun rose over our rimrock Boogie made her decision. She'd resume her duties.

I was thrilled.

We spent time helping her heal and recover her confidence. At night, when her dreams descended into whimpering and crying nightmares, I'd gently wake her with a reminder that she was safe.

Once again, my wife and I were in a tough spot. Crimson's fear issues weren't getting better. Sam wasn't ready to take on high desert predators by himself and we needed to finish our fall grazing to stay out of our ledger's red ink.

On a ranch, arguments between dogs happen, however an unprovoked attack is a different matter. During long conversations in the evening, we decided to buy time until winter weather drove us to our feeding pens. We kept guarding and herding dogs separated, even though it made our work more complicated. We hoped it'd prevent another explosive situation. As an added benefit the chaos of our house construction would be closer to completion.

Two months later, we were still incident free. Slowly, we relaxed. Our new system seemed to be working, even as Crimson continued her wary ways.

Then, it happened again.

Boogie got separated from the others when Crimson jumped her. We were better prepared this time and our strong and immediate response broke up the fight. There were no injuries requiring a veterinarian.

After the dogs were separated and the dust settled, my confidence transmuted into profound sorrow. I glanced at my wife and asked, "Do you remember our agreement if this happened again?"

She nodded and turned away. Tears catching the evening light.

Decisions like these are never simple, nor easy. We had no good options. It was our time to stare in the eye, without flinching, at the reality of our world and see it as it really was, rather than the way we wanted it to be.

Crimson, the aggressor, was an aging and emotionally crippled livestock guard dog who'd never allowed our human touch. She was nearing the end of her working life. Boogie was in her prime. She was an experienced, competent and confident stock dog. On any given day, she'd have happily turned herself inside out to please us.

The following day, a fall storm was kicking up to our west. Lowering clouds made the mountains look like lopped-off sandbox constructions. The wind was fitful and fallen aspen leaves danced circles in our yard...

> *...what do you say*
> *to a dog who doesn't understand*
> *why they need to die –*
> *clouds thicken and thunder rumbles,*
> *rain drops fall into tiny puffs of dust...*

...Crimson's end was quick, final, and over. One at a time, we allowed the rest of our dogs to sniff the result. We felt they needed to come to their own understanding of the situation.

My wife said, "Goodbye, Crimson, we'll miss you, pretty girl. You tried hard to work through your fear, but just couldn't get the job done."

Finished, we buried her in the special spot we reserve for good dogs.

> *...we finally had our answer: we'd never know what it was like to take Crimson's big head in our hands and feel her large body relax into our arms.*
> *When working with livestock every day, it's possible to feel the general mood of animals in the barnyard. Are they relaxed? Nervous? Tense? Maybe frustrated or frightened? Much like walking into a room or an elevator filled with people, it's an easy task to determine the livestock's emotional state of mind.*
> *The following day, Crimson's fear was gone from our barnyard. We'd become so used to it, we hadn't realized it was there. The relief was powerful and heart felt. Working together, we began the healing process and supported Sam in his new...and lonely...lead guard dog role with our flock as Winter approached.*

[to be continued on page 72]

CHAPTER 4
A Cry for Help

ATLAS...

Since he got out of the military, DL has a new lease on life.

If asked how that happened, he'll give tons of credit to his service dog Atlas.

"Just like his namesake in Greek mythology," says DL, "Atlas is the one who carries the weight of the world on his shoulders. In this case, I'm his world."

This former combat medic with post traumatic stress disorder (PTSD) has come a long way since his fighting-to-survive days. He has a new job, the best relationship with his kids he's had in a long time and, while his nightmares haven't quit, his buddy Atlas watches over him when he sleeps.

He says, "Every night, the nightmare is always the same. Just when the pain, blood and violence of my dream are at their most intense, some character in the dream will reach out and lick me in the face. You know that doesn't happen in combat, this is so far from the reality of war that it'll yank me out of my dream state, and I'll lay there in bed, breathing and heart rate recovering, with Atlas' nose inches from my face as he licks me again. I can't possibly describe the amount of pain those nighttime licks have saved me. He's my buddy."

By any measure, it's tough for a nightmare to survive the anxious and attentive slurping tongue of a dog. But Atlas' service isn't finished when the sun halos the mountain in the east.

They have a meeting with a half dozen veterans who are candidates for their own PTSD service dogs. For DL it's an appointment, a heartfelt labor of giving back, but for Atlas...

Hugging a Dog

It's show time.

One by one, the veterans file into the reception area. Their eyes are all the same, a mixture of pain colored slightly with the tiniest inkling of hope. They bear the body language of an abused dog in an animal shelter that's been returned more times than it can count and watches everyone who comes in the door, hoping against hope. Each veteran is…*WAY*…outside his comfort zone.

"Hi, my name is DL and this is my service dog Atlas," he says, pointing to the dog laying between his feet.

Introductions and a brief military resume is offered. Each relaxes slightly as they realize everyone in the room has been through a similar situation and speaks the same language. Even so, their eyes are constantly moving, aware and assessing. While sitting, they are balanced on the balls of their feet, aware of tiny sounds in other parts of the office.

Atlas lies calmly between DL's feet, eyes closed. He's not sleeping, but radiating calm and aware of everything going on in the room.

Each of these veterans made a choice to take a chance and seek a better life. They're not sure what's involved. The conversation ranges far and wide, but the questions always return to service dogs…

"How do I get through an airport and into the plane with a dog? Do they treat you OK?"

"What about restaurants and places where
they have trouble with phony service dogs?"
"How do you get a dog on an escalator, and will
they be OK for my kids at home?"

In some cases, reassurances are made. In other cases, it's..."we'll cover a lot of that as you and the dog get used to each other, you'll need to walk your walk and when you run into something you're not sure how to handle, contact the other vets in your group and we're here to support you."

Throughout the entire time, Atlas, eyes still closed, continues to radiate calm.

DL is a private person, but he understands how to work with the public. His conversation can be animated when he's trying to make a point and his volume picks up slightly.

Each time the conversation gets a little more intense, one of Atlas' deep, brown eyes will pop open and he'll glance at DL to make sure everything is still OK. If DL's voice is sharper than usual, Atlas will sit up, scanning his face until he's assured that all is well. When that's over, he lays down and closes his eyes once again, radiating calm the entire time.

As each veteran steps back into the office with the service dog trainers, DL says, "Don't worry, me and Atlas will be with you the rest of your five weeks of training. If you have any questions or run into any problems, we'll get it handled."

...at this writing, DL and Atlas have been working together for just over a year.

In many ways, DL's life has improved measurably since that relationship began. But life happens. Bills need to be paid, work intrigues must be dealt with, and there are too many things to be done. Plus, there are still times, especially at night, where he's unable to keep his mind from going to..."that dark place."

When that happens, he relies on his buddy to...'have his back'...and give him a big, juicy dog slurp when he needs it most.

That makes a bad day better.

DIESEL...

*The rural American West is working dog country.
Digging a reluctant bull out of the brush,
making a long and harrowing run gathering spread-
out livestock or working dawn until after dark trotting
alongside the boss' horse is what it takes. They get their
job done and earn their kibbles that night.
However, working dogs do more than gather
cattle or put sheep in the proper pen. Sometimes, their
job is simply to be a companion for someone with a need.
When that happens, the dog is in the right spot...*

Diesel, the dog, looked for a moment when the professor's back was turned to the class. He tiptoed to an empty desk in the rear of the classroom. Hopping into the seat, he turned and faced the front of the class with the rest of the students.

That's a good thing, it means he's no longer in a tough spot.

Years before, as a puppy in a different home, from the first moment he was in his element. His new owners were a grief-stricken young couple who'd lost their much beloved elder dog. Diesel stepped into the gap, bonded with the people and they formed a family where he made a new life.

As an adolescent, this youngster traveled to work with the wife at the dog groomers. He was the one happily riding behind her bicycle in a baby trailer. There, he spent his day sleeping, eating, and playing with the others in doggie daycare.

He was the center of attention and that was OK with him.

As Diesel matured, he graduated from riding in the baby trailer to behind-the-bicycle jogger and newspaper delivery dog. His specialty was retrieving thrown papers that had missed their mark for a second...hopefully, more accurate...toss. He was growing into an intelligent and personable dog. In his canine mind, there was no doubt the world was his friend.

A Cry for Help

"He is about the best dog I've ever had," the wife said.

That's when the threads of Diesel's life unraveled.

The husband got a job in remote Montana. For him, it was an excellent career move. However, housing options were minimal, and job demands immediate. They located one rental house. Diesel's owners were thrilled, and they jumped at their new life. All too soon, they found the reason for the opening, it came with unavoidable and irreconcilable landlord issues.

"I think you better find another place to live," said their landlord.

A tiny apartment was the next landing spot for Diesel and family. There was no yard and no welcome for a young and active dog. The rental agreement specifically stated...

"No Dogs Allowed!"

...mediation, dog damage deposits and pleas were no help. The dog had to go.

Diesel was in a tough spot. His owners had a choice between a home for themselves or getting rid of their buddy. Excuses wouldn't be tolerated.

Frantically searching for an option, it seemed to the owners as if there was no room for a dog that was everybody's friend. Diesel had a deadline that would change the rest of his life.

On the day before his reckoning, Diesel's owners heard about a university professor who was in her own tough spot. Her husband had died just before Christmas and within days of putting down one of her two beloved dogs. In the space of a couple weeks, the professor's life had been shattered.

"I thought about adopting from the pound," she said, "to help me and my remaining old dog with our grief."

Two young dogs had applied for the empty spot in the professor's life. However, the elder dog...the canine Queen Mum, so to speak...had rejected the youngsters. For the professor, the oldster's acceptance was paramount.

On Diesel's big day, within 24 hours of homelessness, the young couple gave him a tearful goodbye and sent him across the state to the professor. For them, he traveled with a wish and a hope.

"The first thing I noticed about Diesel," the professor said, "was that my old dog backed away less rapidly than she had with the previous two dogs."

She continued, "Then I realized he was well trained, had good manners and loved people. These qualities were important to me."

Once again Diesel stepped into the gap in a human's life. He turned up the volume, full force, on his winning personality and aimed it directly at the professor.

It worked.

These days Diesel slips into the classroom whenever he can, melting anxious student hearts with his charisma. At the university, any circle of cooing and admiring students is likely to have Diesel, at ground zero, as the center of attention.

In class, whenever he's in their midst, student attendance is higher, and they are more relaxed. This is a plus for everyone, including the professor...*especially*...before a test. Should attention wander away from the dog, he'll crawl back into an empty desk and oversee proceedings from there.

Diesel has made a new life and is in his element. For a dog, that's a good place to be.

> *...that following summer, after school was out, Diesel accompanied the professor on photography expeditions around the rural American West.*
>
> *Since that time, the professor has retired from teaching to a tiny mountain town. She picked up part-time work as a photographer at the local newspaper. Diesel and the professor travel together while she takes photos of small-town sporting events, civic meetings and politicians who kiss babies.*
>
> *There is no word yet about Diesel melting any politicians' hearts, but we figure it's a matter of time.*
>
> *Besides, for a dog, it's a good place to be.*

BLACK DOG WITH NO KNOWN NAME...

Some dogs find their place in this world, others never do.

This next story is an open letter to the former owner of a dog that was dumped in our area. I wanted that person to understand what happened to this animal.

I felt they needed to know the rest of the story...

Dear Former Dog Owner:

I'm sure you recall your dog. She was a little black mutt, no taller than your knees. Her hair was short, and I doubt she weighed more than a medium-sized bag of dog food.

You, like many others, probably hoped she'd find a good home when you dumped her along our road. Ranchers have their own dogs; and don't need more. Most times a dumped animal finds a harsher end through disease, starvation or getting run over. The fate of your little black dog was somewhere in between. She found some kindness, but no home.

A Good Samaritan found her along the highway and coaxed her into the back of his pickup. Trying to locate her owner, he stopped by our Post Office.

She jumped out and disappeared from view.

For weeks that little black dog hung around our tiny ranching community. She ate stolen dog food when she could find it and from garbage cans when she couldn't. She was always a fleeting shadow disappearing around the corner.

You hadn't cared enough to spay her, so when it was her time, she came in heat and attracted the attention of a local Golden Retriever. Together they ran and ran and ran.

When I first saw your little black dog, she was so skinny her ribs were sticking out. She and the male crossed town, traveled over a ridge, and ended up in our sheep pens. Neither dog was interested in our sheep. However our guard donkeys

unsuccessfully tried to kill the both of them. Fortunately, neither was injured.

We phoned the male's owner, and he arrived a few minutes later. He thanked us and apologized for his dog. As neighbors do, we chatted. He filled us in on the doings of your little black dog. We discussed how a timid, plain-colored dog has little or no chance to be adopted at an animal shelter, especially when pregnant. Her physical condition was obviously deteriorating and we agreed it was time to take the situation in hand.

In most cases, when the public adopts a dog at the pound, they choose a brightly colored, friendly or well-socialized animal. Sometimes, they'll head straight to the cute puppy pens. Your little black dog wasn't a bad dog, but she fit none of these categories. In the shelter, she would have been more of a 'project' dog with fear and trauma issues. Yet another strike against her finding a new home.

Two days later, I was fixing fence when I heard running hoof beats. I looked up and saw the Golden Retriever running for his life in front of our guard donkeys. Teeth bared and ears flat back, they chased him under a fence.

We called the male and chained him in our yard. I went in the house to get a rifle. Every so often, I'd get a glimpse of your black dog slinking through the shadows worrying about her friend.

She circled closer and I waited for an opening...

> *...hope steps away when*
> *a dog sees its death*
> *in your eyes –*
> *whispering: "I'm sorry,"*
> *doesn't change a thing...*

...I did the deed that needed to be done. I didn't like it very much, but it may have been the kindest thing to ever happen to your little black dog.

So, that's what happened to the dog you dropped off that day. I did your dirty work and made myself responsible for the mess you allowed to happen. Just so you know, I'm signing this letter with no respect for you at all.

Bing Bingham

...this hard story has been heard on the radio and published around the country. Public reaction has been resoundingly positive. However, there was one comment that meant more to me than all the others.

Each fall a neighbor drives his cattle from their high-country meadows past our place on their way home.

On this day, the weather was miserable and a ranch hand I barely knew stopped the drive in the muddy road in front of our house. He waved me over to our front gate.

With rain dripping off the brim of his soggy cowboy hat, he said, "I wanted to thank you for writing that story about the black dog."

"Thanks," I said, "but, why's that?"

"Because more people need to know how things really work in ranch country. Keep up the good work."

Folks, touching someone's heart is a rare and sacred thing in this business...ESPECIALLY...when you're standing in a crappy old rainstorm.

HALF-STEP...

Feral dog packs are a thing.

When dogs are neglected, abandoned, or ignored, sometimes they collect in a pack and revert to their primal natures. Their lives become about dominance, sex and avoiding starvation.

Dog cannibalism creates a food opportunity when resources are scarce. Anything that runs...wildlife, pets, livestock...can be their prey. There are documented incidents where they've preyed on small or solitary humans.

Many years ago, there was a story about a young girl in elementary school. On most days, she got off the bus with her friends and they would all walk to their rural homes. On this day, for whatever reason, she was alone and vulnerable. The local dog pack found her and gave chase.

The pack wanted what any feral dogs want. If they'd eaten recently, she was a play toy far a bored pack. If hungry, well, you get the idea.

The little girl never found out exactly what the pack intended. She survived by climbing a tree. There she sat while the pack milled around the base and voiced their frustration. Her frantic parents found her unharmed, but very scared some hours later.

That little girl is a grown woman these days. We don't care to speculate on the nature of her dreams at night.

This next story starts with a pack of dogs on an Indian reservation, they could have been from anywhere. They were doing what feral dogs do best, trying to stay alive...

The puppies didn't have long to live.

Their mother was an unusual dog. She was an alpha female who wanted nothing to do with humans. When she came into heat, males from near and far showed up for the occasion.

No one knows who won the prize, it might have been the most dominant or the smartest and sneakiest. It probably doesn't matter as puppy litters can have more than one biological father.

But the female knew how her world worked:

If her lactation could be stopped...most likely, by the death of the pups...then she'd return into estrus and be ready for breeding again. This is a marvelous adaptation for the survival of a species, but it's really hard on the puppies caught in the middle.

She was smart and experienced at this game. Her priority was the survival of her puppies.

When birth was imminent, she dug an earth den. In places it was over four feet deep, a deterrent to the males trying to kill her pups. There were numerous caverns in her den. She would use these as bolt holes in case another area was compromised. All the tunnels were barely larger than her so she couldn't be outflanked in a fight.

Her big day arrived.

Afterward, when the pups were asleep, she'd silently slip out of the den and dash off to find food for herself. Quickly, the puppies nursed and grew. Soon they began making little mewling and growling noises.

Gradually, the neighborhood males became aware that... *something*... was going on in her den. Still, she'd slip out for a quick bite and return to her nursing and guarding duties.

The little ones grew. Before long, the sounds and smells were undeniable and the fight with the males was on. She no longer dared leave her den. The puppies were still nursing and pulling on her physical reserves. She needed food. With resources dwindling, her race against time soon wouldn't matter. She'd need to make a choice between her life and the little ones.

As time passed, her life was reduced to minimal nursing, daily skirmishes, and dog fights at the entrance of the den.

That's when the rescuer got a phone call from neighbors who'd heard the ruckus. It didn't take long for her to assess the situation. If the pups were to live, their circumstances needed to change.

Crawling on all fours, the rescuer explored the den as deep as she could feel. The tiny hungry puppy sounds were

A Cry for Help

beyond the end of her fingers. Knowing she needed to work quickly, she excavated as far as she could reach into the den.

Near dark, she found three of the bigger pups. Quickly, she gathered them into a dog crate and put them in her car. Hurrying home, she deposited them in her puppy nursery.

She knew the next day would be difficult.

The remainder of the pups were deeper in the den. However, accessing their hiding place would require more underground exploration, leaving her exposed and unable to defend herself from an overly excited dog pack.

That night, she fed her family a late dinner and made phone calls to get help for the next day. She slept with prayers for the mother dog and the remaining pups on a long night.

The following day, the rescuer and her helper arrived at the den and the renewed sounds of excavation attracted the pack. One armload after another, helper watching her back, she scooped dirt from the den. Before long, her rear end and legs were the only parts of her sticking out of the ground.

Deeper in the den, she found two terrified pups huddled in a dirt nook. She lunged and grabbed, then passed them to her helper to put in the crate.

Still, she could hear the whimpers of one puppy coming from the dark recesses. Silently, she listened. Unable to dig deeper, she used her hands to feel deep into the openings.

Nothing...still, she could hear tiny whining sounds.

Frustrated, she asked her helper to bring a cell phone. Turning on the camera and flash, head deep in the den, she took pictures of every underground cranny in front of her.

First photo - nothing but darkness.
Second - no puppies there.
Third - not here, either.
Fourth - nope, not here.
Last one - *THERE HE IS!!*

Around a corner, where she could barely reach was a terrified puppy cowering and crying in the dark...

...c'mon home
the next step is a big one,
filled with
gentle hands and clear eyes –
someone wants to say, "Hello"...

...jamming her face into the dirt wall, she pushed and grabbed the squealing and squirming puppy. As the rescuer shimmied backwards out of the den, she looked down and saw it was missing half of its left rear foot. Last pup secure in the crate, the rescuer and her helper drove home.

For the first time in weeks, the dog den was quiet. The puppies were safe. Each appeared healthy, except the last pup with a half paw. A closer look showed a physical deformity rather than an injury.

Socialization with humans is a big deal for feral puppies. All but one...the last pup with the deformed foot...adored human attention. His personality was much like his mother's, aloof and uninterested in people. The rescuer worked with him, but he wasn't interested in treats, attention or people. He didn't care. She knew finding a home for him might be difficult.

Weaning time came and the rescuer posted pictures on social media and asked folks if they could think of interesting names.

Her phone rang, it was her stepdad.

"Do you see that pup on the end, the one not looking at the camera?" he asked. "His name is Half-Step and I want him."

The rescuer wasn't sure what to say. Her stepfather hadn't owned a dog in twenty years. He seemed interested, though.

"You're sure?" she asked, listing his socialization issues.

"He's my boy and I want him," he said.

She made that happen.

A 500 mile trip across the state...the pup still uninterested in anyone...and she deposited Half-Step into her stepdad's arms.

The pup came alive. He looked at his surroundings with interested eyes, especially her stepfather. The youngster couldn't get enough of him. He settled into his arms and let out a contented sigh.

It'd been a long journey along a scary road, but Half-Step had come home.

...weeks later, Half-step is settling into his new home. He's interested in taking walks anywhere her stepfather wants to go. He's a young, strong and active dog.

A year later, it's tough to separate Half-Step and her stepfather.

The dog weighs about ninety pounds and he's the light of her stepdad's eyes.

TAZ...

A gangly, raw-boned young dog stared through the animal shelter window. He was hoping for a second chance at life.

No one knows for sure what this dog's first chance looked like. It probably wasn't horrible, no excessive beatings or long-term neglect. Someone put time into him, and it showed. For a youngster, he was well mannered.

Most likely, he'd been purchased as a cute puppy. That attraction wore off about the time his boredom and back-yard escapes began. After one-too-many escapades, his first owner...probably...just never bothered to pay his bail and reclaim him from the pound.

Makai walked in the animal shelter door, the dog sat quietly and watched.

"This is Cheetoh," the assistant said.

'What a silly name for a beautiful animal,' Makai thought. The dog continued watching, barely blinking.

Many dogs, at this stage in their lives, are frantic for acceptance.

They leap, bark, wag their tails and, often, make a nuisance of themselves. Seeing through that abundance of excitement is part of Makai's job. He's a facilitator for a program assisting juvenile offenders in gaining self confidence through the care, maintenance and training of a dog. When finished, the dog is adopted to a waiting family.

Not every person or dog makes the cut to get into this program. Of those who do, most have never experienced unconditional acceptance. For them, canine or human, Makai is their second chance at life.

This dog in the shelter showed none of the usual excitement. He sat and watched. Makai took his lead and they walked to the shelter's exercise yard. There, they played. For a young dog, he was calm, but bright and responsive.

'Taking this dog into the program is a no-brainer,' Makai thought and said to the shelter assistant, *"Of course, we'll take him."*

He had just the young man in mind who might be interested in training this animal.

"I've always wanted a dog like that," the young man exclaimed, "but I want to change his name to Taz."

That was Thursday, the day Cheetoh became Taz...

On Friday morning Makai went to work and headed for the dog kennels. He paused and said "Hello" to the newest trainee. He went about his day, but found himself repeatedly veering in the direction of the dog runs and inquiring of Taz's new trainer about the animal's care and his paperwork.

Each time Taz wasn't involved in training demands, he watched every move Makai made. The kennel staff noticed. However, the object of Taz's attention was oblivious.

At the end of the day Makai was ready to go home when a couple of volunteers pulled him aside. They explained what they'd observed and told him it might be a good idea if he took the dog himself.

His reaction was quick, "NAW! No way." 'I don't have time for a dog right now,' Makai thought.

Makai was going through a rough patch in his life. Some months before, he'd put his favorite old dog down and split up with his wife, then his father died. He felt like his innards had been pulled out. Nearly every emotional button had been torn loose. His heart was an open wound, bleeding, raw and painful.

Months later, his pain slowly dimmed. As a coping device, he decided his life would be easier just doing the "guy" thing, alone and by himself. He'd be fine and if someone didn't believe him, all they need do was ask him and he'd explain he was fine, thank you very much.

Makai relaxed and changed his mind, he said, "Maybe, I'll just take him home over the weekend."

The entire trip home, Taz watched as Makai drove. When they arrived, the dog walked into the house and immediately fit into the daily routine. His manners were excellent and he was completely house trained. His sons were thrilled with the addition...however temporary...to their home.

To be fair, there were some close calls when Taz got near the chicken coop. Makai let him know, right quick, that stalking the inhabitants wasn't acceptable behavior.

For a couple days they weren't sure the dog would understand they didn't want him chasing chickens. However, for Makai this was non-negotiable. On the third day of Makai's long weekend, Taz..."got it"...and, for the dog, the chickens no longer existed.

Conflicted, Makai returned to work knowing in his heart he wanted the dog, but his head told the story that it 'might' work.

Arriving he sought the young man who'd named Taz. Not knowing what reaction to expect, he explained the situation and how he thought Taz might work out as his dog.

The young man's smile brightened the room. He said, "No problem, he's a good dog. You keep him. I'm going to be in here a long time and can always get another dog. Besides, did you think I didn't notice how he was always watching you?"

Makai smiled as he drove home that night while Taz watched from the passenger seat.

...Makai and Taz are still together. Their active lives... skiing, hiking, camping, swimming...revolve around each other. He says, "I've never seen a dog who enjoys swimming completely submerged as much as he does... the first time he did it I was really starting to worry before he came back to the surface."

Months later, there's news...
One day the duo were walking through a nearby community when Taz disobeyed a command and caught the attention of a bake shop owner. Apologizing for his dog, Makai met a single mother who also likes dogs. Their conversation went on.
"I can't believe it," he says. "She's someone I can talk with for hours without pretense or effort."
Makai doesn't know where this budding relationship is going. He's pretty excited, though.

And a year after that, there's more good news...
Makai and the bake shop lady are married now. They and their dogs Ruby and Taz are doing just fine.
So, please folks, give Makai a gentle and kind thought as he rebuilds his life...with Taz's help...into his own second chance.

LIVESTOCK GUARDIANS CYCLE
Holding a Dog's Head - Part 3

SAM, KEENA and ARCHIE

Months went by and the storm winds of winter blew us from the dark season of Crimson's death.
What we didn't know at the time is there was a livestock guardian puppy waiting in the wings. Her name was Keena. She was looking for a job and ready to come running.
That following spring...winter's trauma finished...Sam stepped into his roll of being our confident lead guard dog. It was turn-out time.
Grass was growing, Meadowlarks were claiming their nesting territory and the range was filled with young animals. Scent posts needed checking, there were new game trails to be investigated and, maybe best of all, winter-kill carrion to be savored...

When Keena arrived on the scene, she was focused on her new situation and filled our barnyard with bubbling puppy energy. It seemed as though forty percent of her body weight was her huge paws and great floppy ears that, sometimes, dragged on the ground.

When Sam was tired of her leaping at his face or hanging from his ears, he'd hold her down with one paw while she squealed with delight. There was no doubt in her mind that she wanted to be the best apprentice livestock guard dog ever.

Sam accepted her.

We watched him slip into his teaching roll as the rest of her body caught up with her ears and paws. She grew into a large and beautiful dog. He showed her all the best scent posts and she was happy with 'second-sniffs' and learning the guardian game. Each night, the two would return to the pen knowing chow was coming...

...great toothy grins,
dusty tails helicoptering –
two dogs trot
across the rocks for food, rest
and, best of all, us...

...after gulping their chow, both dogs pressed their heads against our thighs, requesting hugs, ear rubs and scratching for any itchy spot where warming weather loosened their fur.

With pleasure, we indulged them.

As Keena filled out, she turned into a sleek, muscular, hundred-plus pound dog. Her tail curled tightly over her hips, and she carried it like a flag in a VFW parade. However, what stood out was her bark. It'd leave your ears ringing. Our joke was that it could trigger rock slides in our surrounding hills.

Keena had been with us for a couple of years. She'd reached her full physical size, but not the maturity of a confident livestock guardian when she had her first incident.

I wasn't at the house when my wife heard alarm barks from both dogs in our livestock pens. They'd noticed a young neighbor dog had bumbled its way onto our ranch. The

Hugging a Dog

newcomer wasn't looking for trouble, nor was she hurting anything. She was bored and hoping to find someone who'd play.

Hearing the ruckus, my wife set her coffee on the counter and hurried outside. Her first thought was about a cougar that had previously passed through our area. She grabbed her ATV, loaded her stock dogs on the back deck and headed out to check the problem.

She found the confused young neighbor dog on the outside of our pen worrying about our guard dogs on the opposite side of the fence.

Moving slowly, my wife called to the stranger and reached her hand out to be sniffed. Then, as the dog relaxed, she gave it a reassuring ear rub. Meanwhile, quietly detaching a horse lead rope from her ATV and clipping it to the youngster's collar.

"We need to find your home, little one," she said to the frightened young dog.

Each of our stock dogs has been trained to jump up

and ride on the back deck of an ATV. The strange dog didn't understand that command. She sat on the ground quivering with fear.

My wife turned to her dogs and said, "Alright you two, scoot your butts over and make room for this one."

Favoring her bad knee, she picked the youngster up and placed him with the other two. It was much like lifting a soggy, wriggling forty-pound noodle. It didn't work well...plus...there was some age-induced grunting and groaning uttered by my wife.

Behind the fence, Keena thought the sounds of discomfort meant the stranger had hurt my wife. She went ballistic. Her alarm barks ratcheted up to rage.

She threw her muscular body against our pen fence until it broke. Between one heartbeat and the next, she charged and knocked the frightened stranger flat, tumbling her across the ground in a ferocious display of canine dominance and threat.

Keena had truly taken over Crimson's old spot as 'the enforcer.'

My wife changed the tone of her voice to that of a senior pack alpha and projected all of her authority into her command:

"KEENA...NO!!!"

Keena was growling her threat and standing over the young stray like an avenging angel. The youngster lay still and silent, doing her best not to tempt fate.

My wife continued her own dominance display, catching and holding Keena's eye with her own. At the same time, she reeled the sprawled youngster in with her catch rope and pinned the frightened animal between her calves and the ATV. Not wanting to be the center of attention in a four-dog fight, she turned a gimlet eye on her worried stock dogs that were still perched on the ATV. "You two, stay put and don't move!"

Keena was circling the ATV and the youngster crammed against the foot rest, waiting and watching. The only sound was a deep rumbling from her chest. Her body language indicated acceptance of my wife's authority. But she was ready to renew her argument at any moment. Neither dog offered to take up the issue. Slowly, the canine confrontation stabilized. The youngster was shaken and frightened, but uninjured.

Maintaining dominant eye-contact with Keena, my wife

picked up the youngster...*making sure to keep silent this time*...and plopped her on the ATV deck, keeping a tight grip on her collar. Still wary, Keena was no longer in a red zone rage. She circled the ATV as my wife made her way towards our barnyard.

By this time the ruckus had caught my attention.

I met my wife and we checked the stray for injuries that might have been missed...nothing broken nor bleeding. However, we had little doubt the young dog would be stiff and sore in the morning. We gave her water and an armful of straw to lay on in our enclosed metal stock trailer.

Just before returning to the house, my wife said to the youngster, "Yeah, I know, little one, you didn't deserve that. Let me see if we can get you back home."

In the house, we rewarmed my wife's coffee and made a cup for me. Sitting by the wood stove, we compared notes. Both of us hoped the excitement was done for the day.

It was later that night when the stray's owner came to collect her wandering young dog.

...Keena had been doing her job the best way she knew how, we never punished her for that aborted attack.
So we're back to Sam, the keystone of our guard dog program.
These days Sam is showing his age. He prefers

the softest and driest bed at night and doesn't like getting his paws muddy in the Spring rains unless, of course, he's cooling off on a hot summer day. Then he enjoys a dip in a nearby algae covered stock pond. We can always tell when that happens because he comes home with green smears half way up his chest that looks much like a dog's dirty bathtub ring. On slow, predator-free days, he'll bring home a half rotted deer leg for evening snacks. Still, he'll back Keena up every time they encounter a predator.

We'd like to retire him to the position of yard guard for his own safety. However, he's refused each of our attempts. He ends up making our lives and his own miserable until we let him back out with the livestock...

Then we heard about some folks who had a young male livestock guard dog available. They came well recommended from an area, much like ours, where cougars are the problem.

We made a deal and brought the pup home. His name became Archie.

Keena accepted the youngster after she realized he was no threat to her dinner dish. Sometimes she'd clumsily play with him when no other dog would.

For Sam's part, he wasn't sure why we'd brought another

pup home for him to raise. He dialed the youngster out of his life and ignored him.

Slowly, over several months, Sam came to accept him. There were times when we'd see Sam patiently standing, hoping for one of us to save him from the youngster that was begging to play or hanging by his teeth from Sam's ruff.

Archie watched Sam and Keena as they went about their guarding business. He learned well.

Slowly, Sam dialed back his custom of being the first with a warning bark announcing something strange in the neighborhood. Keena picked it up. Before long, Archie was out there with the other two giving warning barks to all predators that this area was protected by three big dogs.

Our local predators knew their limits, and, for the sheep and goats, life was good. But, perhaps best of all, each of our dogs loves to have their head hugged when they see us during our evening feeding. It's hard to say who enjoys it more, us or them.

As 2020's summer cooled into fall, Sam was showing his age with signs of limping and stiffness. He was still alert and happy to be here, just moving slowly. During evening chores, we began offering him the option of stepping through the gate and into the yard. Then we started feeding him there. Soon he realized, he liked sleeping in the duff next to our haystack and getting extra attention in our yard. However, when he realized he got to lick out our cast iron dinner cookware like the stock dogs, then he was sold on the retirement deal.

During the day, while the weather is still relatively mild, he likes it when we let him out of the yard to be with his buddies in the sheep pen. In his mind, he probably feels he's giving the two younger guardians guidance in their duties. In reality, he spends much of his time asleep in a comfortable spot out of the wind.

Then during evening chores, he's all too happy to come back into the yard. He wouldn't dream of walking up those scary porch stairs or coming into the house. That's more than he's willing to do.

...while his retirement is still a work in progress, we're glad to know it's unlikely this former coyote and cougar skirmisher will be caught out alone where he's unable to defend himself. Plus, we get to hug his large head while his tail slowly waves back and forth like a flag in a parade and tell him how much we appreciate the work he's done over the years.

And besides, who wouldn't love a big white dog that keeps deer out of the lilacs?

CHAPTER 5
Sure Eye, Strong Heart

BOOGIE...

This next story is about a dog that will always have a place in my world.

In the working stock dog world, it's generally accepted that it's a good idea to start them off slow. That way they gradually become accustomed to the needs of their new working life, In other words, don't put a youngster in a dangerous or more chaotic situation than they can handle. A bad or frightening experience can negatively impact the rest of their working life.

When starting a new pup, I follow that rule and let the young dog build their confidence at their own pace. However, sometimes the dog's confidence has nothing to do with my time frame...

It was chore time in our hog pens.

We keep one separate pen for breeding the sows to our boar. Then we let nature take its course and almost four months later, we're the proud owners of a new litter of piglets.

On this day, our boar and one sow were patiently waiting for their food. However, the other sow, for some unknown reason, was in mid-snit. She didn't think we were moving fast enough with...'her'...food.

Hogs are among the most intelligent animals in the barnyard. Like humans, they have good and bad days. In this case, the sow in question figured a hissy fit would motivate us to hurry with her chow.

As experienced livestock people we knew better than to let a 500 pound animal with the strength of a small bulldozer win the...'*Who's in Charge?*'...question in a high decibel temper tantrum. In most cases, we use our stock dogs as enforcers. Growling, snarling and snapping, they hold the critter off their food until we say they can have it...*VOILA!*...dominance

80

reestablished and the situation is defused.

However, this sow was having none of it. She'd hustled her quarter-ton rear end to a corner in her hut and held the dogs off with her slinging head and slashing teeth.

In most cases, my wife's lead stock dog Tango, a strapping sixty pound male, handles these situations. He's a formidable beast who doesn't put up with a lot of back talk.

But, he was in trouble. Every trick he tried ended with him staring into her thigh-bone crushing mouth filled with teeth. She outweighed him by almost ten times. For him, it would have been suicidal to go in that hut and he knew it. The situation was getting dangerous. The sow was winning and she knew it. My wife and I consulted outside the pen.

Boogie was a youngster, less than a year old, and weighed no more than a medium size bag of dog food. She was excited by the action and wanted to be a part of it. I held her in my arms to prevent her from getting injured and ruining her confidence.

Tango was doing his best to figure a way past the hog's sharp teeth to her rear end where it was safer.

Boogie relaxed in my arms and waited until my attention was elsewhere, then she exploded into the air and leaped the hogpen fence before I could call her back. Darting past Tango, she checked to make sure the sow had been distracted. Then, using her small size to advantage, ran underneath the slashing jaws, between the sow's legs and chomped her on a tender flap of skin.

Taken by surprise, the hog screamed and leaped straight in the air nearly tearing the roof off her cozy, low-slung hut. Returning to Earth, she wasn't sure what'd happened, so she escaped at high speed for the safety of the other hogs at the far end of the pen. In her haste, one of her legs clipped Boogie, rolling her end over end.

Spitting desert dust and hog pen duff, my little dog and Tango hastened that sow on her journey to safety.

With all parties uninjured and safe, we told the two dogs...youngster and boss dog...to hold those hogs in the far end of the pen until they calmed down. Once that happened, the hogs had done what we requested for long enough, so we called the dogs out of the pen and rewarded the hogs by feeding them.

Training stock dogs is much like any other dog, it takes a combination of repetition, praise and reinforcement. Both dogs returned from the pen when called. We praised them and made believe they had successfully completed...no matter how unplanned on our part...a training exercise.

...I confess, I was proud of Boogie that day. After all, with her inexperience it could have so easily gone a different way. I told her she was a good dog, gave her a quick pat on the shoulder and we went off to finish the rest of chores.

But that set things up for her to be an extraordinary livestock and companion animal. For the next decade, we put in a lot of miles together. As I write this, she's asleep on her rug in my office.

BOOGIE AGAIN...

Remember Boogie?

She was the youngster who sailed over a fence to put a cranky hog in her place. She's also the one who was so badly injured when our out-of-control livestock guardian singled her out. (page 50)

In between, she and I've traveled a good many miles together. She's the dog that, when I put a camera to my eye, will sit directly behind me so as to not mess up that photo. When the camera comes down she goes back to sniffing the interesting smells.

This isn't something I've taught her. In fact, before I knew what she was doing, I'd step backwards and stumble over her. Frankly, that was cause for a few exciting moments between us.

And that's what we were doing during this final story. She was my photographer's assistant while I'd been assigned to take pictures at a horse-drawn equipment auction...

My ears were ringing with the auctioneer's chant. The smell of greasy corn dogs and over-cooked pizza clogged my nasal passages. There were too many things to see and I was worn out.

It was time to take a break, so I headed for the parking lot.

Leaning against the seat in my pickup's open door, I sipped water and nibbled on my stashed granola. My dog jumped out of the truck.

"Tired of sitting?" I asked. "How about we take a walk and clear both of our heads?"

I slipped a rope leash over her head, more for the sake of the people around me than any need on her part. As we walked, I tucked the end of her rope through one of my camera backpack straps. She trotted by my side and sniffed her way through the equipment aisles.

That's when the old-timer noticed us and said, "You got a pretty good handle on that dog."

"Thanks," I replied. "We've spent a lot of time together and have taught each other pretty well."

I continued, "I got her from a hired man who worked on a ranch deep in the desert. When she was a pup, it took me a month to convince her there were more than four humans on the earth. After that, we bonded pretty tight."

The old-timer had long-distance blue eyes that looked more comfortable navigating a ridge than stepping into a city crosswalk. His salt and pepper beard was so long that it probably caught any crumbs spilled while eating beside a campfire. He knew how to introduce himself to a stock dog. Bending over, he let her sniff the back of his hand. When she was finished, he squatted to her height and scratched her back.

Boogie is usually standoffish with strangers. I was surprised when she didn't summarily dismiss him. Rather, she leaned into his attentions while keeping an eye on his facial expressions.

He said to me, "When my last dog was a pup, I took her and my mule into the Colorado mountains for four months. She didn't know anything other than me and that mule. That's when a person learns to relate to a dog..."

...me, you and a mule
the whole world, just us–
wind tickled pines
beneath the Milky Way
our home, family, everything...

...he continued, "Thanks, I appreciate you letting me love on your dog for a while. You know, I think I'll get one more dog to see me out of this life."

"Good luck to you," I said.

We wandered off in a separate direction through the crowd.

A few minutes later, Boogie and I stepped aside from the ebb and flow of auction traffic. I hunkered down and she turned to face me, wondering what I wanted. I gave her one of her favorite ear rubs.

"Thank you for giving a lonely old guy his dog fix," I told her.

She stared back, ears erect and head cocked. By her body language, I understood the old-timer was in the past. She was more concerned about finding a rat or squirrel to hunt somewhere in a forgotten corner of the auction.

I smiled back at her and we moved back into the crowd. There was at least one of us hoping to spot that rodent.

...moments of grace are a rare thing in this world. Dogs are better than humans at creating these special times.

These days, Boogie is showing her age. Her fur is getting tufty, her hearing isn't what it was and she spends more time on the rug near the wood stove. I try not to laugh when a rodent gets away from her these days.

When her time comes, that's fine. We've had a good long run and I'm content with our adventures together. And yes, when that happens, I'll probably get another dog to see me out of this life.

So that's where things stand at the Dusty Dog Cafe.

*This book is complete, but the stories aren't over.
They say a story is the shortest distance between two people.
I confess, over the years I've known some excellent dogs and
their stories have come from wonderful people.*

*Researching this book has been...mostly...a
pleasure. There were times when the view in my mirror
was uncomfortable. However, it was filled with self
knowledge. Any fear, laughter or quiet sobbing in the corner
is for ourselves and the world we've created. Each time,
we...'get'...a story, it's because it resonates in our heart.
That's the power of story.*

*The dogs in this book live in the modern, rural
American West. Each of them has made mistakes, messes or
been caught goofing off. They are neither one hundred percent
hero nor bad dogs. They are, or were, somewhere in between,
doing the best they can with what was available.*

*Please know that I tip my ball cap in respect to the
owners who trusted me with their dog's story, even when
it was embarrassing or painful to recall. I hope I've been
authentic and true to their experience.*

*None of this would have happened if it wasn't for
you, the reading and listening public. Without you, not nearly
so many people would know a piece of these dog's lives. Those
of us at the Dusty Dog Cafe's long table, where the locals
swap stories and cuss or discuss their world over an endless
cup of coffee, hope you've enjoyed them.*

We'll talk again...

AUTHOR'S NOTE...

"Hey, where's the Dusty Dog Cafe? I can't find it anywhere."

That question comes up a lot. Well, not to be cryptic, it's everywhere and nowhere. The Dusty Dog Cafe is an imaginary construct existing only on the web. However, the idea is based on hundreds of small town coffee shops around the rural American West.

They're not hard to find.

Simply follow the main drag through a farming or ranching town and look for the restaurant where the locals gather. You'll know it by the dusty cars or flatbed pickups - usually with a stock dog or two in the back - parked nearby.

Step across the sidewalk around the wooden benches. No one worries about sitting outside in the nice weather, because there's not enough traffic to be bothersome. Peer through the gingham-draped windows at the large, mounted deer, elk, antelope or bison.

Inside, the booths are usually made of wood and circle the walls. In the center of the room is a long table where the locals - business people and local officials who are taking a break, crusty retirees without much to do, farm or ranch wives and their husbands, running for parts or making a day of it in town - gather over an endless cup of coffee to cuss and discuss the events of the day.

It is here, in this tiny coffee shop, a person can hear the stories about dogs that have made a difference around the rural American West. And it's here where yours truly has spent more than his fair share of time, ears flapping and coffee cup in hand, listening to the stories of the people who own those dogs.

These are the stories from the Dusty Dog Cafe. Take another sip of coffee and enjoy the journey - I know I did.

- D. "Bing" Bingham

IT TAKES A VILLAGE...

No book is completed in a vacuum. These are the folks who've been down in the dust and dog hair with me wrestling these stories into submission...

For Jan, long time cheerleader and caller of BS. You were there when needed, it's been a good run old friend. For Nancy and Jerry and the trust of these longtime friends. For Makai, who returned many phone calls and gave more than I ever expected. For Al and Jan who were in the right place and time, then sent me searching in the correct direction. For DL, Kyal and Jona, who were placed in harm's way through no fault of their own, I thank each of you and am humbled by your trust. Between all of us, I think we got it about as close to right as possible. For Paul and Lynn who went above and beyond and for Brin, Kema and Eric, with their eagle eyes and talent for translating my voice into words. For Elizabeth, who came along and saved the day. And for Ann, along for the whole ride...I love you.

For each of you who has a dog that's important in your life, now's the time to reach over and give them an extra ear rub.

Any errors in this book are mine.

D. "Bing" Bingham is a storyteller and retired freelance writer, photographer and public radio producer. For him, it's always been about story, particularly those involving hope and humanity.

For 25 years, he roamed the Pacific Northwest, Northern California and Nevada gathering news and features on rural and agricultural issues for many different outlets. His credits extend from the Smithsonian's National Museum of the American Indian and National Public Radio to numerous regional and local magazines, newspapers, radio stations and websites.

These days, he's still gathering stories around the rural American West for his Dusty Dog Cafe blog. He and his wife live on a small and remote ranch deep in Oregon's high desert with three very dusty dogs.